DRUMSENSE

Author:	Colin Woolway
Editor:	Simon Hedger
Music Illustrations:	Paul Hose
Cover Design:	Xtreme Graphics
Cover Illustration:	Xtreme Graphics
Publisher (This Edition):	H&H Publishing
Producer (This Edition):	Hal Leonard Corporation

DRUMSENSE VOLUME ONE 4ᵀᴴ EDITION

Copyright 1999 H&H Publishing
Published 2003 by H&H Publishing. www.imsestore.com
Produced 2003 Hal Leonard Corporation. 7777 West Bluemound Road P.O. Box 13819 Milwaukee, Wisconsin 53213
Colin Woolway has asserted his right to be identified as the author of this work
Under exclusive license to H&H Publishing Nottingham England
hh.publishing@virgin.net

DRUMSENSE VOLUME ONE 4ᵀᴴ EDITION AUDIO

Copyright 1999 H&H Publishing
Published 2003 by H&H Publishing. www.imsestore.com
Produced 2003 Hal Leonard Corporation. 7777 West Bluemound Road P.O. Box 13819 Milwaukee, Wisconsin 53213
Colin Woolway has asserted his right to be identified as the author of this work.
All rights of the owner of the work reproduced reserved.
Under exclusive license to H&H Publishing Nottingham England
hh.publishing@virgin.net

PLAYBACK+
Speed • Pitch • Balance • Loop

To access audio visit:
www.halleonard.com/mylibrary

Enter Code
5441-1231-2962-8260

ISBN 978-0-634-01004-0

Visit Hal Leonard Online at
www.halleonard.com

Contact us:
Hal Leonard
7777 West Bluemound Road
Milwaukee, WI 53213
Email: info@halleonard.com

In Europe, contact:
Hal Leonard Europe Limited
42 Wigmore Street
Marylebone, London, W1U 2RN
Email: info@halleonardeurope.com

In Australia, contact:
Hal Leonard Australia Pty. Ltd.
4 Lentara Court
Cheltenham, Victoria, 3192 Australia
Email: info@halleonard.com.au

DRUMSENSE

DEDICATIONS

This book is dedicated to my family: My parents, David and Cathy, my brothers Philip and Ian, my sister Judith, my wonderful wife Lucy, and my sons Silas and Finlay. Also a huge thank you to the Zildjian family, for unqualified support — the unflappable Bob Wiczling and Tina Clarke. Special mention to Ian Croft from Sonor and Neil Laviree from Vic Firth, Andy Fox, Bill Sanders, Dean Bowdrey and Ashley Wardell.

Colin Woolway uses Zildjian cymbals, Sonor drums, Vic Firth drumsticks, Aquarian drumheads, Protection Racket cases and Bill Sanders practice pads exclusively.

INTRODUCTION

The material in this book represents the basic coordination needed between your feet and hands to play the modern five piece drum set. The concepts dealt with, although elementary, are incredibly valid. The idea of moving a roll around the drums in various ways is something that will become a completely natural part of your playing. Rolling on the snare drum, picking out subdivisions on the toms and then the cymbals, is something drummers do all the time, in practice as well as playing live or recording. In terms of playing "time," any accomplished drummer would be able to change the hi hat pattern to complement the feel of a song, without having to alter the bass or snare drum pattern.

To get the best from this book, don't just practice the patterns you find easiest, make sure you tackle everything. Remember, if you don't, you can be sure that someone else will.

Find a good teacher to help you get everything right, and have fun!

Best wishes

Colin Woolway

DRUMSENSE COUNTING METHOD

The author believes that examples of music written in 4/4 ought to be counted using numbers 1 to 4 as pulse markers and then sub-divisions "e + a" therein. The reason behind the *Drumsense* counting method of 1 to 8 is simple — during the first lessons in any drummer's career they have enough to fathom without worrying about initially complicated counting methods. For example, when approaching patterns such as BASIC ROCK #3, instead of confusing the student with fractions, i.e. the additional bass drum is on the "+" of 2, wouldn't it be easier for you, the teacher and indeed the student, to simply say, the additional bass drum is on the 4th hi hat that you are required to play.

You will note that on page 18, the book introduces the student to counting using quarter note pulse markers 1, 2, 3 & 4. If you require any further information or help please do not hesitate to contact us at support@onlinedrumstudies.com

Remember, it isn't the author's intent to rewrite music theory, but it is his intent to introduce the world of drumming to any student in a much simpler way to understand and thus provide the student with quicker results.

SPONSORSHIP AND SUPPORT:

The Drumsense teaching program is supported by many of the
drumming industry's leading manufacturers including;

Zildjian	supply high quality cymbals for tuition.
Sonor	supply high quality drum kits for tuition.
Vic Firth	supply high quality drumsticks for tuition.
Protection Racket	supply high quality padded protection for drum kits and hardware.
Bill Sanders	supply high quality silent practice pads and silent drum kits for tuition.
Rockschool	working together with Drumsense to promote and raise teaching standards with GCSE and A-level equivalent qualifications available.

If you are interested in knowing where your nearest Drumsense teacher is, or would like more
information about the Drumsense teaching program, contact Colin Woolway at:

Drumsense Studio: +44 (0) 20 8288 0863

CONTACT DETAILS

DRUMSENSE

68-70 London Road
West Croydon CR0 2TB United Kingdom

H&H Publishing

www.imsestore.com
Tel/Fax: +44 (0)870 130 7432

Hal Leonard Corporation
www.halleonard.com

DRUMSENSE
TUTORS

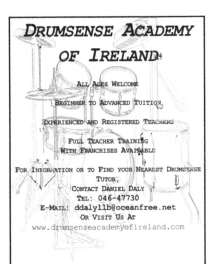

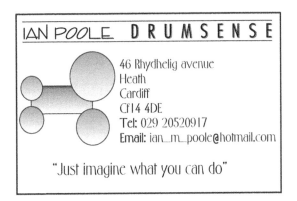

KEY AND FEATURES

SYMBOLS

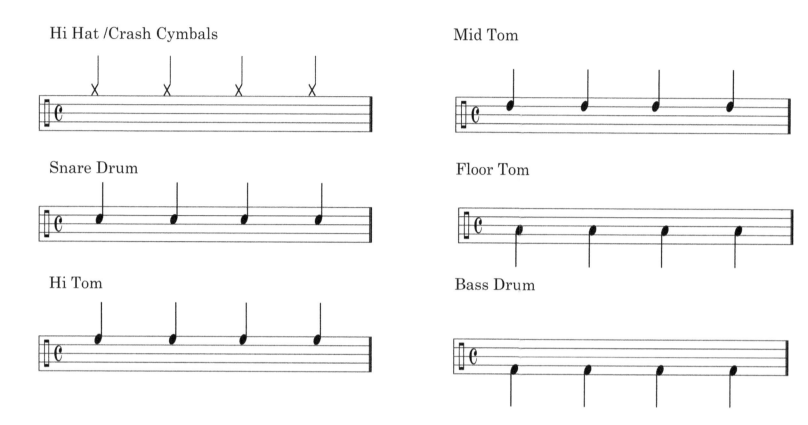

Hi Hat /Crash Cymbals

Snare Drum

Hi Tom

Mid Tom

Floor Tom

Bass Drum

TRACK LISTINGS

Your *Drumsense* volume has accompanying audio.

Each section in the book marked with (Track #) , relates to the audio track.

The number within the symbol tells you which track number the exercise relates to.

Each track covers one example and all its variations.

USING THE AUDIO

You will gain the most benefit from this book by using the audio from the very first page.

This will enhance your understanding of the music, and enable you to hear how the patterns should sound at slow and medium tempos.

Always try to count along with the audio, and listen to each example at least once before attempting it.

CONTENTS
Part 1

Part 2

Part 3

Part 4

DRUMSENSE AUDIO

PART 1

BASIC ROCK

Counting from 1 to 8, play the notes on the Bass Drum and Snare Drum as they appear.

1. The Bass Drum is played on counts 1 and 5, and the Snare Drum on counts 3 and 7.

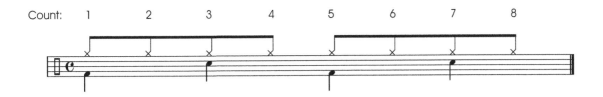

2. Now add a Bass Drum on count 6, so that you have Bass Drum notes on counts 1, 5 and 6.

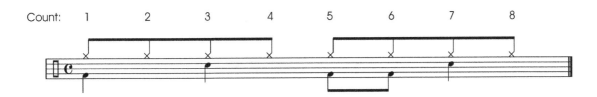

3. Here the Bass Drum is played after the Snare Drum, on count 4.

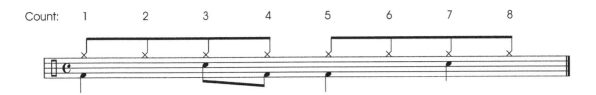

4. Play Bass Drum notes on counts 1, 4 and 6.
This exercise is a combination of ex. 2 and 3, losing the Bass Drum note on count 5.

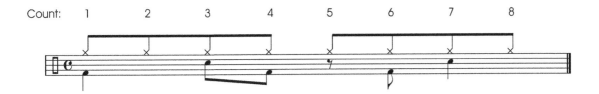

SHUFFLE ROCK

Now we are going to play the same Bass Drum and Snare Drum patterns as we did in BASIC ROCK, but with a "shuffle" or "swing" feel on the Hi Hat. The count for the Hi Hat notes is: 1   + 2   + 3   + 4   +

1. Here the Bass Drum notes fall on counts 1 and 3, while the Snare Drum notes fall on counts 2 and 4.

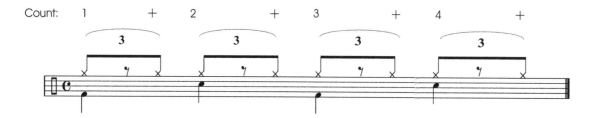

2. Now play an extra Bass Drum note on the "+" count after count 3.

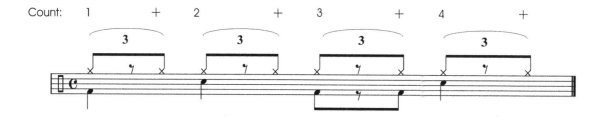

3. Move the extra Bass Drum note back to the "+" after count 2.

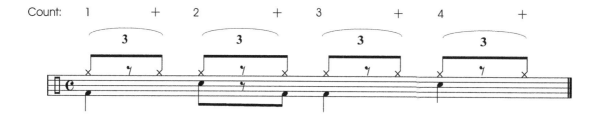

4. Now the Bass Drum notes appear on the "+" counts after 2 and 3.

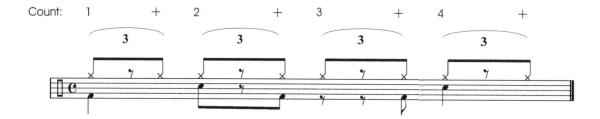

DRUMSENSE

SNARE DRUM INDEPENDENCE

Here we are going to be adding Snare Drum notes independent of the Bass and Snare Drum notes that we have already learned.

1. Count the Hi Hat notes from 1 to 8 as before, but this time add "+" between counts 4 and 5.

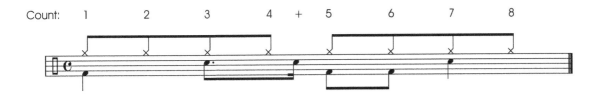

2. Add another independent Snare Drum note between counts 5 and 6.

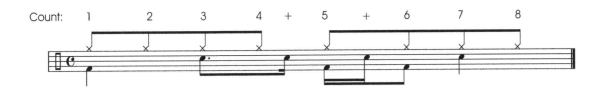

3. Add one more Snare Drum note at the end of the bar, between counts 8 and 1 of the next bar.

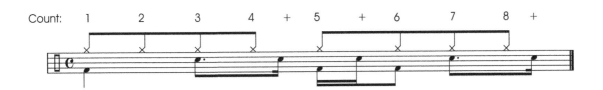

Note: Remember, there is no pause between the "+" at the end of the bar and count 1 of the next bar. Therefore, in order to play two bars, you must count:

1   2   3   4 + 5 + 6   7   8 + 1   2   3   4 + 5 + 6   7   8 +

BASS DRUM INDEPENDENCE

Now we are going to play Bass Drum notes independent of the Snare Drum and Hi Hat notes. Count the Hi Hat in the usual way, and add Bass Drum notes as "+" in the same way as SNARE DRUM INDEPENDENCE.

1. Play an independent Bass Drum note between counts 2 and 3. All the other Bass Drum notes fall on the Hi Hat.

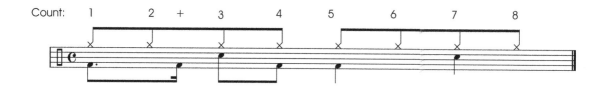

2. Here play an independent Bass Drum note on the "+" between counts 4 and 5. So the Bass Drum notes fall on 1, "+" and 5.

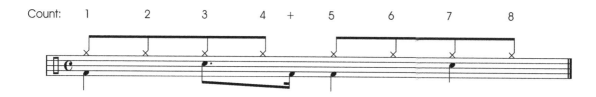

3. Now add an extra Bass Drum note on the "+" of count 3.

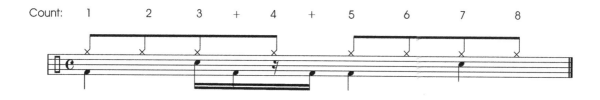

4. Finally, add a Bass Drum note on count 2.

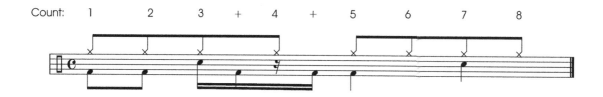

*Note: exercises 2, 3 and 4 are **progressive,** that is, each one is the same as the one before, but with one note added.*

HI HAT INDEPENDENCE

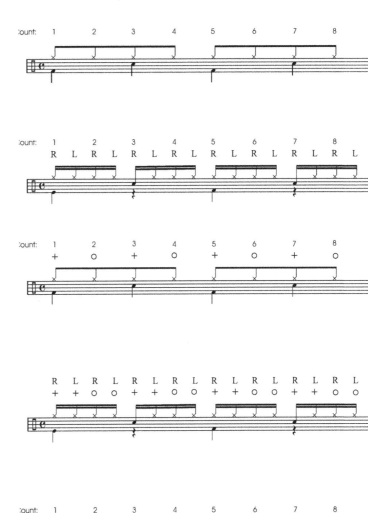

Section 1 - Eighth notes on the Hi Hat

Section 2 - Sixteenth notes on the Hi Hat

Section 3 - Eighth notes on the Hi Hat,
open on the Offbeat

+ = closed o = open

Section 4 - Sixteenth notes on the Hi Hat,
open on the Offbeat

Section 5 - Offbeat Eighth notes on the Hi Hat

The next stage of basic Drum Kit coordination is to practice some different Hi Hat patterns. The best way to do this is to go back over the Bass and Snare Drum combinations that we have already learned, and apply new Hi Hat ideas.

SECTION 1

Eighth Notes On The Hi Hat

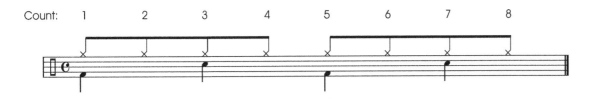

This is just confirming that all the combinations we have just learned are based on playing eighth notes to the bar on the Hi Hat, so move straight on to Section 2.

5

SECTION 2

Sixteenth Notes On The Hi Hat

a) Basic Rock

We have made two basic changes here. Firstly, both hands play on the Hi Hat. Secondly, the Snare Drum note is played with the right hand instead of the left, leaving out the Hi Hat just for that note. Go back to BASIC ROCK, and convert all the patterns from eighth notes to sixteenth notes.

Basic Rock No. 1 with sixteenth notes on the Hi Hat.

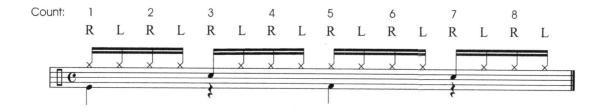

Basic Rock No. 2 with sixteenth notes on the Hi Hat.

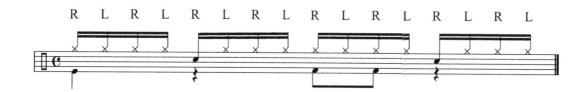

Notice that all the Bass Drum notes still fall under the right-hand Hi Hat notes, as they did when we played eighth notes.

Basic Rock No. 3 with sixteenth notes on the Hi Hat.

Basic Rock No. 4 with sixteenth notes on the Hi Hat.

Sixteenth Notes On The Hi Hat

b) Snare Drum Independence

Continue to play the right-hand Snare Drum notes as before, but play the independent Snare Drum note (the one between counts 4 and 5) with the left hand.

Snare Drum Independence No. 1 with sixteenth notes on the Hi Hat.

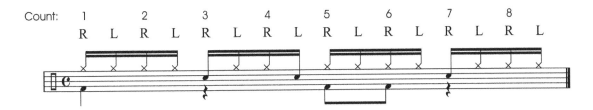

Snare Drum Independence No. 2 with sixteenth notes on the Hi Hat.

Snare Drum Independence No. 3 with sixteenth notes on the Hi Hat.

c) Bass Drum Independence

Here we must get used to playing a Bass Drum note with our right foot, and a Hi Hat note with our left hand at the same time. Any Bass Drum notes that were independent when we played eighth notes on the Hi Hat will now fall on the left hand as we play sixteenth notes on the Hi Hat.

Bass Drum Independence No. 1:
The Bass Drum note on the "+" between counts 2 and 3 will fall on a left-hand Hi Hat note.

Bass Drum Independence No. 2:
The two Bass Drum notes on counts "4 +" and 5 will fall on left- and right-hand Hi Hat notes consecutively.

Bass Drum Independence No. 3:
The Bass Drum note after the first Snare Drum note must fall accurately on the left hand.

Bass Drum Independence No. 4 with sixteenth notes on the Hi Hat.

Eighth Notes On The Hi Hat Open On The Offbeat

Up to now we've been keeping the Hi Hat cymbals firmly closed while we play eighth or sixteenth notes with either the right hand or both hands. By opening the Hi Hat on the offbeat we achieve two things. First, and most obvious, we get a new feel. Second, we start using the left foot which is coming down on the beat so that the cymbals are open *off* the beat.

a) Basic Rock

Basic Rock No. 1:
Open the Hi Hat on counts 2, 4, 6 and 8, making sure that the Hi Hat cymbals are tightly closed on the Bass Drum and Snare Drum notes.

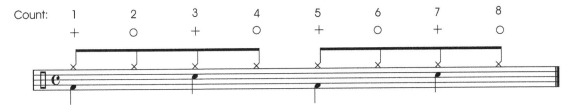

Basic Rock No. 2:
The open and closed action of your left foot must continue as you add the extra Bass Drum note on count 6.

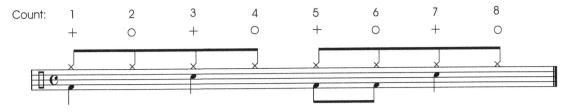

Basic Rock No. 3:
With number 2, the Bass Drum notes fell on a closed and then an open Hi Hat note. This time, you need to play the Bass Drum with the Hi Hat open, then closed.

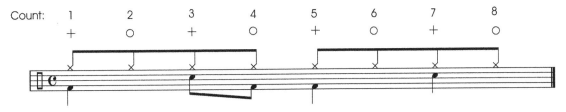

Basic Rock No. 4:
Here, the Bass Drum plays on two open Hi Hat notes. Take care to close the cymbals firmly on count 5.

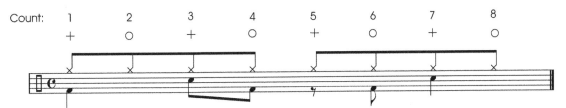

Eighth Notes On The Hi Hat Open On The Offbeat

b) Snare Drum Independence

Snare Drum Independence No. 1:
Be sure to keep the Hi Hat open as you play the independent Snare Drum note. Don't let it close until the Bass Drum note on count 5.

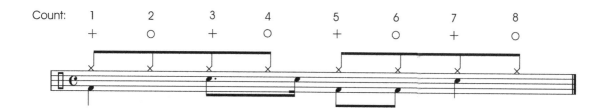

Snare Drum Independence No. 2:
Take great care over the left foot action on the Hi Hat. The first independent Snare Drum note will be played with the Hi Hat open, the second one while the Hi Hat is closed.

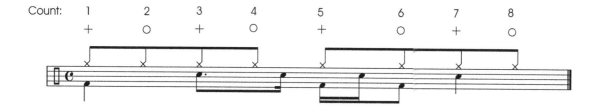

Snare Drum Independence No. 3.

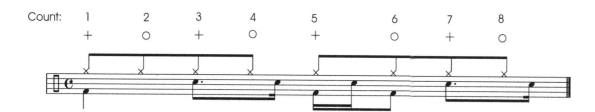

Eighth Notes On The Hi Hat Open On The Offbeat

c) Bass Drum Independence

Bass Drum Independence No. 1:
The Bass Drum note between counts 2 and 3 will be played while the Hi Hat is still open. Close on count 3, with the Snare Drum.

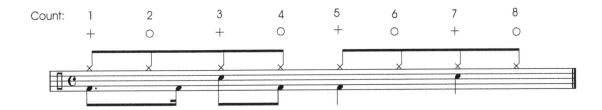

Bass Drum Independence No. 2:
Make sure the Hi Hat stays open for the Bass Drum note between counts 4 and 5. Close for the Bass Drum note on count 5.

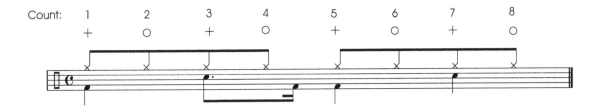

Bass Drum Independence No. 3:
The independent Bass note after the Snare on count 3 is played with the Hi Hat closed.

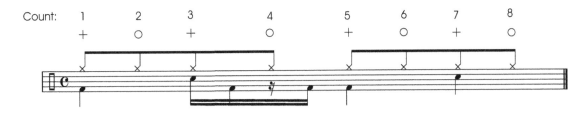

Bass Drum Independence No. 4.

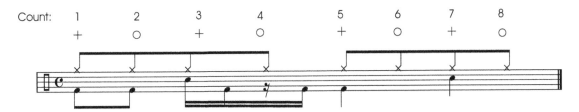

SECTION 4

Sixteenth Notes On The Hi Hat Open On The Offbeat

This is a combination of HI HAT INDEPENDENCE Section 2, and HI HAT INDEPENDENCE Section 3. Your hands play sixteenth notes as in HI HAT INDEPENDENCE Section 2, while your left foot opens the Hi Hat off the beat and closes on the beat, as in HI HAT INDEPENDENCE Section 3.

a) Basic Rock

Basic Rock No. 1:
You will find that the end result of combining sixteenth notes with opening and closing the Hi Hat is that you play the first two sixteenth notes closed, and the next two open.

Remember to play the Snare Drum with your right hand as you close the Hi Hat with your foot.

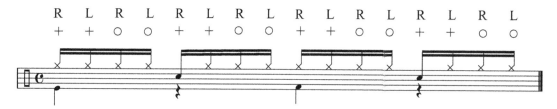

Basic Rock No. 2 with sixteenth notes open on the offbeat.

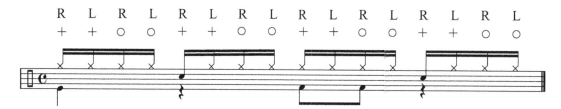

Basic Rock No. 3 with sixteenth notes open on the offbeat.

Basic Rock No. 4 with sixteenth notes open on the offbeat.

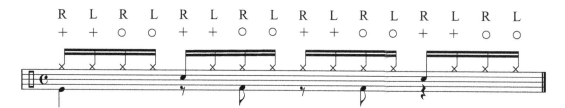

Sixteenth Notes On The Hi Hat Open On The Offbeat

b) Snare Drum Independence

Snare Drum Independence No. 1 with sixteenth notes open on the offbeat.

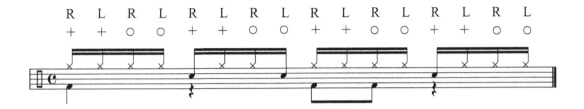

Snare Drum Independence No. 2 with sixteenth notes open on the offbeat.

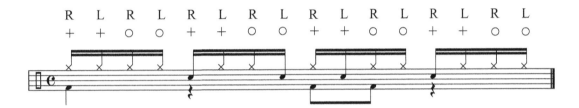

Snare Drum Independence No. 3 with sixteenth notes on the offbeat.

Sixteenth Notes On The Hi Hat Open On The Offbeat

c) Bass Drum Independence

Bass Drum Independence No. 1 with sixteenth notes open on the offbeat.

Bass Drum Independence No. 2 with sixteenth notes open on the offbeat.

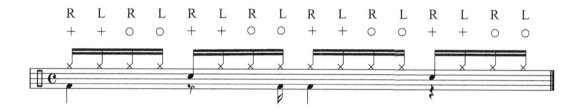

Bass Drum Independence No. 3 with sixteenth notes open on the offbeat.

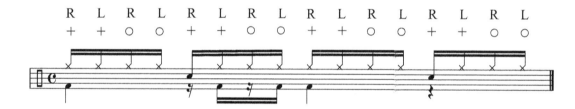

Bass Drum Independence No. 4 with sixteenth notes open on the offbeat.

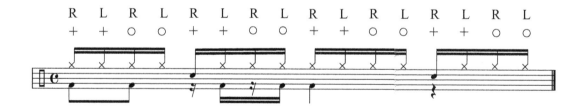

NOTE: There are two possible approaches to Section 4:

1. a) Play eighth notes open on the offbeat, then:
    b) convert to sixteenth notes.

2. a) Play sixteenth notes, then:
    b) open on the offbeat

SECTION 5

Offbeat Eighth Notes On The Hi Hat

By playing every other Hi Hat eighth note, starting on the second, we get a completely new feel to all our patterns.

A good way to play these grooves is to use the bell of the ride cymbal in place of the hi hat.

a) Basic Rock

Basic Rock No. 1:
No Hi Hat, Bass or Snare Drum notes will coincide.

Basic Rock No. 2:
The Hi Hat and Bass Drum notes coincide only on count 6.

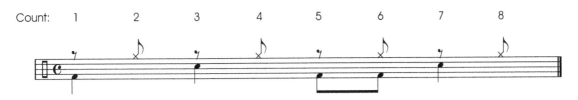

Basic Rock No. 3:
Here the Bass Drum and Hi Hat play together on count 4 only.

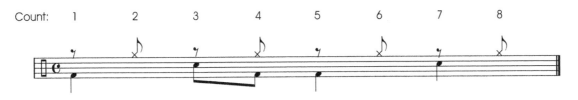

Basic Rock No. 4:
The Bass Drum plays with the offbeat Hi Hat on counts 4 and 6. Count 5 is still in place, but not heard.

Offbeat Eighth Notes On The Hi Hat

b) Snare Drum Independence

Snare Drum Independence No. 1:
Notice that counts "4 +" and 5 are independent Hi Hat, Snare Drum and Bass Drum notes.

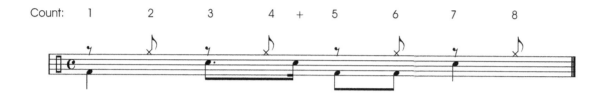

Snare Drum Independence No. 2 with offbeat eighth notes on the Hi Hat.

Snare Drum Independence No. 3 with offbeat eighth notes on the Hi Hat.

DRUMSENSE

Offbeat Eighth Notes On The Hi Hat

c) Bass Drum Independence

Notice here how many notes are completely independent, particularly in No. 3. Take care with spacing and time.

Bass Drum Independence No. 1 with offbeat eighth notes on the Hi Hat.

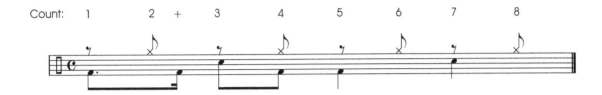

Bass Drum Independence No. 2 with offbeat eighth notes on the Hi Hat.

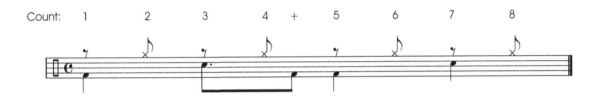

Bass Drum Independence No. 3 with offbeat eighth notes on the Hi Hat.

Bass Drum Independence No. 4 with offbeat eighth notes on the Hi Hat.

PART 2

FILL INS

This part is designed to help you construct "fills" around the Kit. It is assumed that you are using three Tom Toms, two mounted and one on the floor, in addition to your Snare Drum.

If you have only one mounted Tom Tom and a Floor Tom, you will have to double up some of the subdivisions on the Floor Tom. If you have more than two mounted Toms, only use the two most central of them, in conjunction with the Floor Tom, before trying to include them all.

SECTION 1

Subdivisions Of Sixteenth Notes

Subdivisions

1.	**4**	**4**	**4**	**4**
2.	**8**	**8**		
3.	**6**	**2**	**6**	**2**
4.	**3**	**3**	**4**	**6**
5.	**3**	**3**	**3**	**3**

a)   **4**
b)   **2**   **2**
c)   **3**   **1**

Interpretation

a) - Play Around The Kit

b) - Play Accents On The Toms

c) - Play Accents On The Crash Cymbals

Subdivisions Of Sixteenth Notes

a) Play Around The Kit

No. 1. **4 4 4 4**:
Play four single strokes on the Snare Drum, alternate hands, right hand first. Repeat this on the High Tom.
Now play all sixteen notes around the kit without a break as you move from one drum to another.

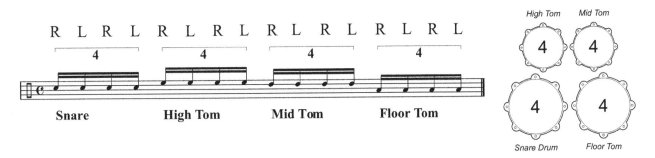

Exercise:

Select a pattern from BASIC ROCK that you are comfortable with, play it three times without stopping, then
play the fill. This is called a *four-bar phrase*.

Example:

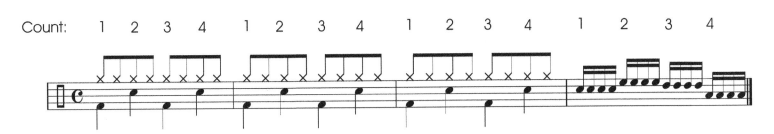

No. 2. 8 8:

Play eight alternating strokes on the Snare Drum, and eight on the High Tom.

Play as a four-bar phrase.

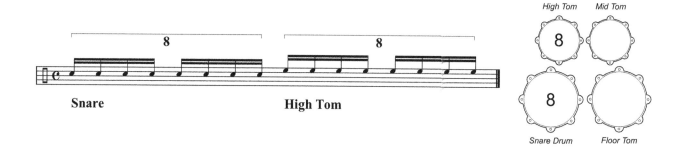

No. 3. 6 2 6 2:

Play six strokes on the Snare Drum, and two on the High Tom, six on the Mid Tom and two on the Floor Tom.

Play as a four-bar phrase.

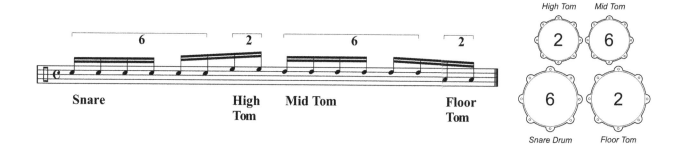

No. 4. 3 3 4 6:

Play three alternating strokes, starting with your right hand, as usual, on the Snare Drum. Notice how you have to start with your left hand on the High Tom to play the next three strokes. Then your right hand leads on to the Mid Tom to play the "four," and also on to the Floor Tom to play the "six."

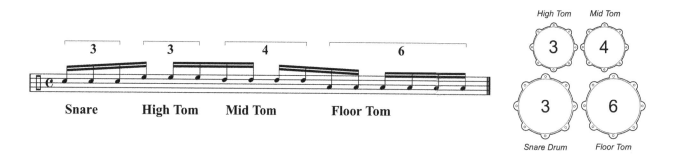

No. 5a. **3 3 3 3 4**:

This time we are going to move backwards as well as forwards around the kit. Play three on the Snare Drum (right-hand lead), three on the High Tom (left-hand lead), three on the Mid Tom (right-hand lead), three on the High Tom (moving backwards, left-hand lead), and four on the Mid Tom.

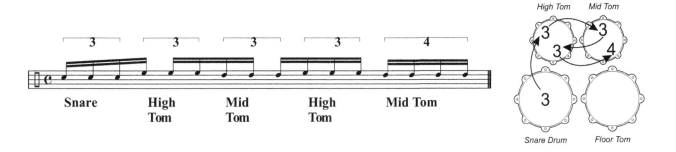

No. 5b. **3 3 3 3 2 2**:

Repeat the sequence of four groups of three (Snare Drum, High Tom, Mid Tom, High Tom, alternate leading hands), but break the "four" from the previous exercise into two groups of two, played on the Mid Tom and Floor Tom.

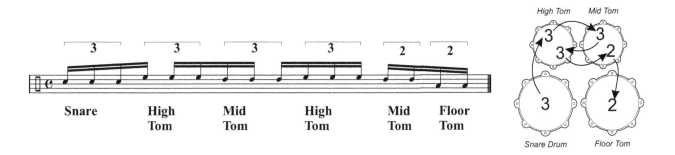

No. 5c. **3 3 3 3 3 1**:

Three on the Snare Drum, three on the High Tom, three on the Mid Tom, three back on the High Tom, three back on the Mid Tom, and one back on the High Tom.

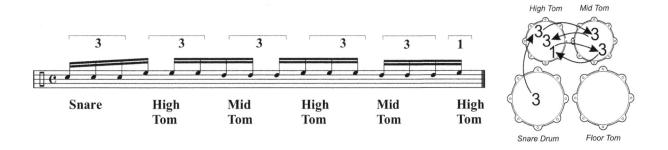

Subdivisions Of Sixteenth Notes

b) Play Accents On The Toms

For this section we are going to go back to the beginning (4-4-4-4), but we'll interpret the patterns in a different way. Play the first stroke of each subdivision as an accent ">," that is, louder than the other strokes. Then play the accent on a Tom, and the other notes on the Snare Drum.

So the first pattern, **4 4 4 4**, will be played as:

    4 = RIGHT-hand accent on the High Tom, left right left on the Snare Drum.

    4 = RIGHT-hand accent on the Mid Tom, left right left on the Snare Drum.

    4 = RIGHT-hand accent on the Floor Tom, left right left on the Snare Drum.

    4 = RIGHT-hand accent on the Mid Tom, left right left on the Snare Drum.

No. 1. **4 4 4 4**:
Play the first of each group of four on a Tom, and the other notes on the Snare Drum, moving the accents around the Kit each time.

No. 2. **8 8**:
Play the first accent on the High Tom, and the following seven strokes on the Snare Drum. For the second accent, try using the Floor Tom, followed by seven Snare Drum strokes.

DRUMSENSE

No. 3. **6 2 6 2**:

6 = Accent on the High Tom, five strokes on the Snare Drum.

2 = Accent on the Mid Tom, one stroke on the Snare Drum.

6 = Accent on the Floor Tom, five strokes on the Snare Drum.

2 = Accent on the Mid Tom, one stroke on the Snare Drum.

No. 4. **3 3 4 6**:

Play the first accent on the High Tom, and the following two notes will mean that your left hand is free to play the next accent.

As the High Tom is the most accessible at this point, use it rather than crossing over to the Mid Tom.

The Mid Tom can be used for the accent to start "four," and the accent for "six" will be on the Floor Tom.

No. 5a. **3 3 3 3 4**:

The accents should flow from the right hand to the left. Try this sequence:

3 = Accent on High Tom, (right hand).

3 = Accent on High Tom, (left hand).

3 = Accent on Mid Tom, (right hand).

3 = Accent on High Tom, (left hand).

4 = Accent on Floor Tom, (right hand).

No. 5b. **3 3 3 3 2 2**:

3 = Accent on High Tom, (right hand).

3 = Accent on High Tom, (left hand).

3 = Accent on Mid Tom, (right hand).

3 = Accent on High Tom, (left hand).

2 = Accent on Mid Tom, (right hand).

2 = Accent on Floor Tom, (right hand).

No. 5c. **3 3 3 3 3 1**:

3 = Accent on High Tom, (right hand).

3 = Accent on High Tom, (left hand).

3 = Accent on Mid Tom, (right hand).

3 = Accent on High Tom, (left hand).

3 = Accent on Floor Tom, (right hand).

1 = Accent on High Tom, (left hand).

Subdivisions Of Sixteenth Notes

c) Play Accents On The Crash Cymbals

Use exactly the same sticking pattern as in part b) Play Accents On The Toms. The accents will be played on Crash Cymbals instead of Toms. *It is very important that every crash is backed with a Bass Drum note.* If you have two Crash Cymbals (or more), try to designate one for right-hand accents and one for left. If you only have one Crash, but you also have a Ride Cymbal, use the Crash for left accents and the Ride for right. *Be careful! Never play a full-blooded crash on a Ride Cymbal.* If you only have one cymbal (crash or ride), use it for right-hand accents, and improvise on the Hi Hat with your left hand.

No. 1. **4 4 4 4**:

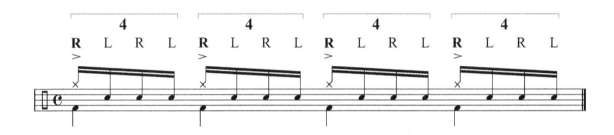

No. 2. **8 8**:

No. 3. **6 2 6 2**:

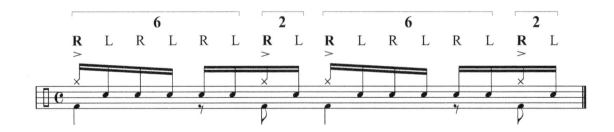

No. 4. **3 3 4 6**:
Remember that the first accent will be played with the right hand, and the second with the left.

NOTE: this is almost the same movement used in BASS DRUM INDEPENDENCE No. 1, with Sixteenth Notes on the Hi Hat.

No. 5a. **3 3 3 3 4**:
Accents flowing from right-hand Crash to left-hand Crash.

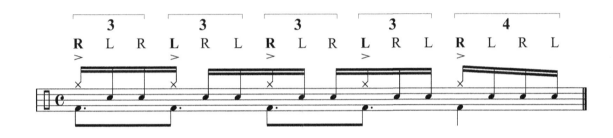

No. 5b. **3 3 3 3 2 2**:

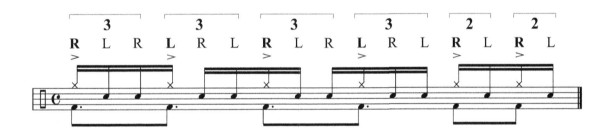

No. 5c. **3 3 3 3 3 1**:

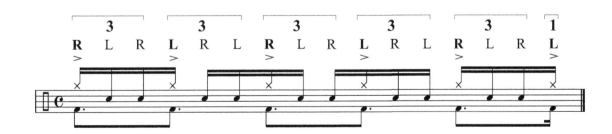

NOTE: The last accent is played on the left hand. If you play a Crash as the first note of the next bar, this will mean two Crashes played left and right, the same movement as BASS DRUM INDEPENDENCE No. 2 with Sixteenth Notes on the Hi Hat.

The second part of this chapter will deal with playing fills in *SHUFFLE ROCK* feel.

These are quite different from the kind that we have played up till now, as they are based in groups of three instead of groups of four (see Subdivision Of Sixteenth Notes No. 1.)

We will use the same approach as before, taking five basic ideas and applying **sections 1, 2** and **3** to each one.

Subdivisions Of Eighth-Note Triplets

Subdivisions

1.	3	3	3	3		
2.	6	6				
3.	6	2	2	2		
4.	2	2	2	6		
5.	2	2	2	2	2	2

Interpretation

a) - Play Around The Kit

b) - Play Accents On The Toms

c) - Play Accents On The Crash Cymbals

Subdivisions Of Eighth-Note Triplets

a) Play Around The Kit

No. 1. 3 3 3 3:
Play three strokes on each drum, taking care to alternate the leading hands as you move from one drum to another.

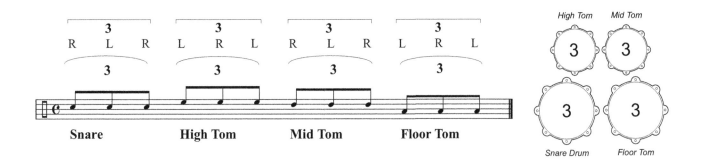

No. 2. 6 6:
Play six strokes on the Snare Drum, then six on the High Tom.

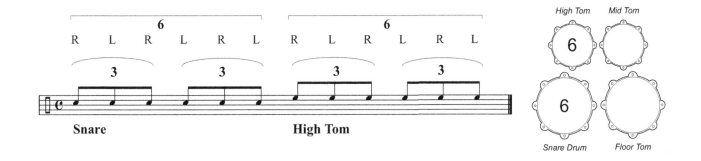

No. 3. 6 2 2 2:
Play six on the Snare Drum, then move down the Toms in even groups of two.

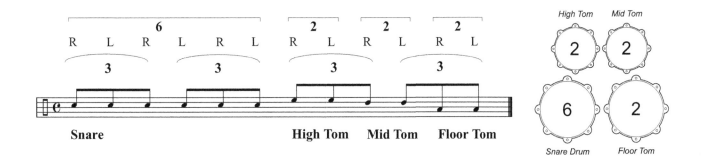

No. 4. **2 2 2 6**:

Start on the Snare Drum, and play three groups of two, ending with one group of six on the Floor Tom.

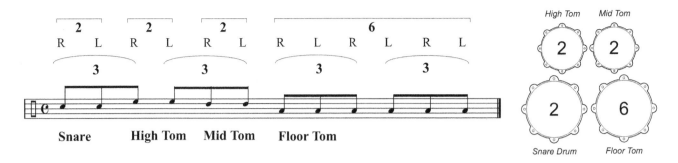

No. 5. **2 2 2 2 2 2**:

This exercise will not work unless you are using five Tom Toms as well as a Snare Drum, in which case you can move around your whole kit in groups of two.

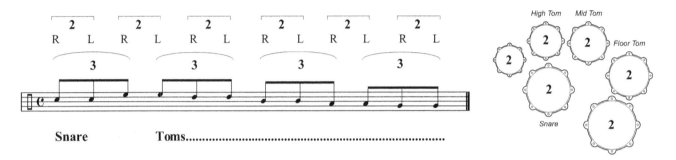

Subdivisions Of Eighth-Note Triplets

b) Play Accents On The Toms

No. 1. **3 3 3 3**:
Play the first note of each subdivision on alternating Toms, and all the "in between" notes on the Snare Drum, as in Subdivisions Of Sixteenth Notes. Remember that the accents will go from right to left each time.

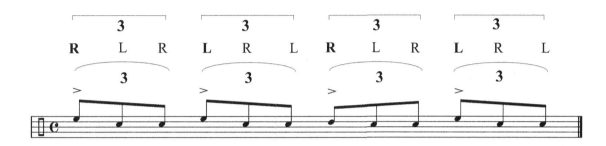

No. 2. **6 6**:
Both the accents here will fall on the right hand.

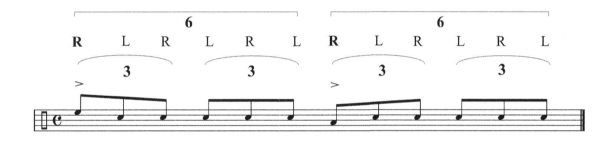

No. 3. **6 2 2 2**:
All the accents here will fall on the right hand. Listen to the accents produced by the right as you play in groups of two. *These are called **Quarter-note triplets***.

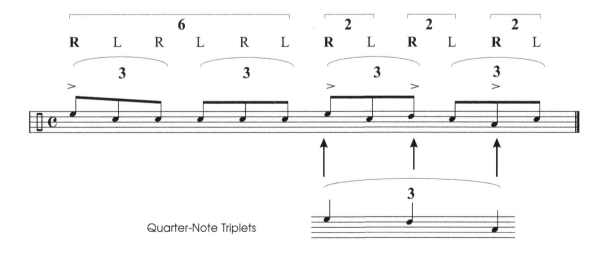

Quarter-Note Triplets

No. 4. **2 2 2 6**:

Think of this fill as four tom accents: **three** Quarter-note triplets and **one** accent at the front of the group of six.

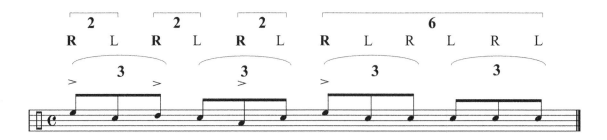

No. 5. **2 2 2 2 2 2**:

The right hand plays Quarter-note triplets around the Kit.

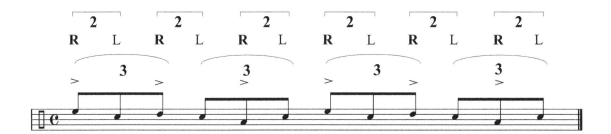

Subdivisions Of Eighth-Note Triplets

c) Play Accents On The Crash Cymbals

No. 1. **3 3 3 3**:
Remember to play the Bass Drum along with each Crash Cymbal.

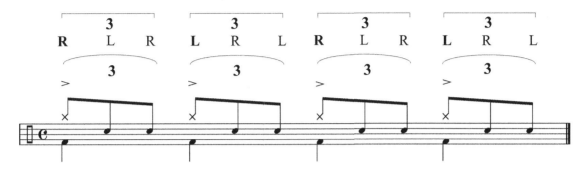

No. 2. **6 6**:
Both Cymbal Crashes will fall on the right hand.

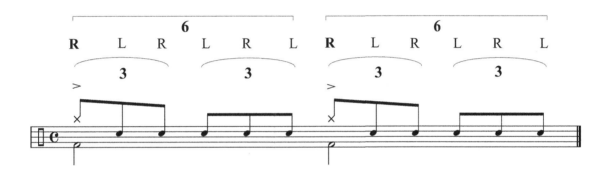

No. 3. **6 2 2 2**:

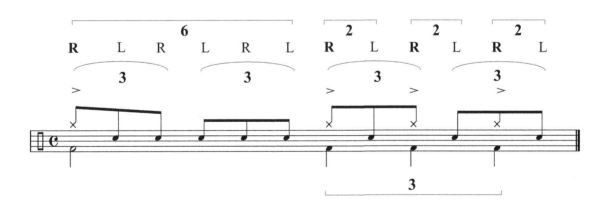

No. 4. **2 2 2 6**:

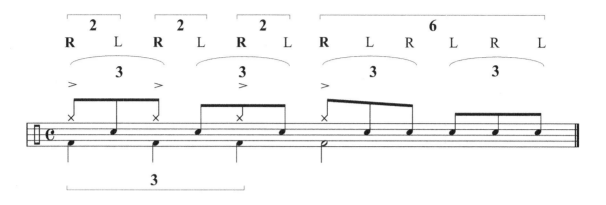

No. 5. **2 2 2 2 2 2**:
The right hand plays Quarter-note triplets on Crash Cymbals. *Try alternating between whatever cymbals you have.*
Don't forget the Bass Drum.

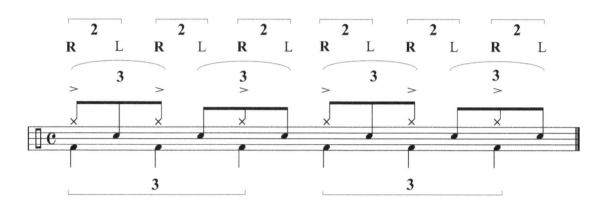

PART 3

RUDIMENTS

Rudiments are often referred to as the *scales* of drumming, and have evolved around the techniques and patterns used by marching drummers over many years.

Although we are not learning to play the marching "parade" drum, it must be acknowledged that we cannot go much further without understanding some basic rolls and practicing the required "sticking."

Following are fourteen of the twenty-six standard rudiments:

1. Single Stroke Roll

2. Double Stroke Roll (or Long Roll)

3. Five Stroke Roll

4. Six Stroke Roll

5. Seven Stroke Roll

6. Eight Stroke Roll

7. Nine Stroke Roll

DRUMSENSE

8. Ten Stroke Roll

R R L L R R L L **R L**
                  >   >
R R L L R R L L **R L**
                  >   >

9. Eleven Stroke Roll

R R L L R R L L R R **L**
                     >
R R L L R R L L R R **L**
                     >

10. Thirteen Stroke Roll

R R L L R R L L R R L L **R**
                        >
L L R R L L R R L L R R **L**
                        >

11. Fifteen Stroke Roll

R R L L R R L L R R L L R R **L**
                            >
R R L L R R L L R R L L R R **L**
                            >

12. Paradiddle

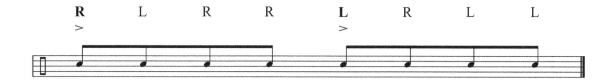

13. Double Paradiddle

14. Triple Paradiddle

PART 4

...AND FINALLY

Track 37 is a short drum solo. It is comprised entirely of the grooves and fills covered in this book. For example, BASS DRUM INDEPENDENCE No. 1 and BASS DRUM INDEPENDENCE No. 4 are both in there somewhere, as are most of the Subdivisions Of Sixteenth Notes, played in all three different ways. *Notice how some of the fills are strung together to make long rhythmic patterns. This is the basis for improvisation.*

Rather than playing along with the whole solo, try working out small sections at a time.

See if you can recognize:

    a) BASS DRUM INDEPENDENCE No. 1.

    b) BASS DRUM INDEPENDENCE No. 4.

    c) Subdivisions Of Sixteenth Notes No. 1, Played Around The Kit.

    d) Subdivisions Of Sixteenth Notes No. 3, with the Accents On The Cymbals.

    e) Subdivisions Of Sixteenth Notes No. 2, followed by No. 4, with the Accents On The Cymbals.

Have Fun

Colin Woolway

H&H Publishing

Would like to thank :

Colin Woolway

Mark Scanlan

Jack Hedger of Able Technical Services
abletech.services@virgin.net

Rob Reid @ Magnet Studios
www.magnetstudios.co.uk

Zach Holt & Laurence Kirk from
Mesters Recording Studio
fudgesabbath@hotmail.com

Dafydd Bevan of Xtreme Graphics
www.xtreme-graphics.co.uk

Thank you,

Simon Hedger   *Paul Hose*

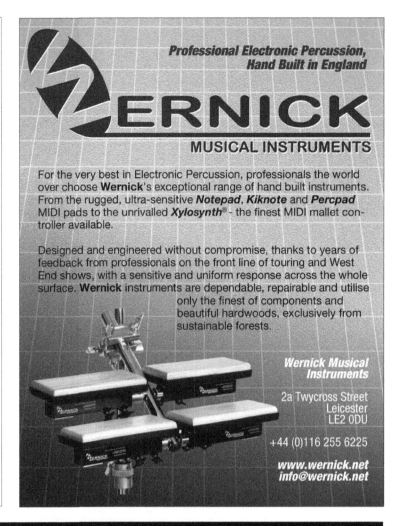

YOU CAN'T BEAT OUR DRUM BOOKS!

Bass Drum Control
Best Seller for More Than 50 Years!
by Colin Bailey
This perennial favorite among drummers helps players develop their bass drum technique and increase their flexibility through the mastery of exercises.
06620020 Book/Online Audio $17.99

The Complete Drumset Rudiments
by Peter Magadini
Use your imagination to incorporate these rudimental etudes into new patterns that you can apply to the drumset or tom toms as you develop your hand technique with the Snare Drum Rudiments, your hand and foot technique with the Drumset Rudiments and your polyrhythmic technique with the Polyrhythm Rudiments. Adopt them all into your own creative expressions based on ideas you come up with while practicing.
06620016 Book/CD Pack $14.95

Drum Aerobics
by Andy Ziker
A 52-week, one-exercise-per-day workout program for developing, improving, and maintaining drum technique. Players of all levels – beginners to advanced – will increase their speed, coordination, dexterity and accuracy. The online audio contains all 365 workout licks, plus play-along grooves in styles including rock, blues, jazz, heavy metal, reggae, funk, calypso, bossa nova, march, mambo, New Orleans 2nd Line, and lots more!
06620137 Book/Online Audio $19.99

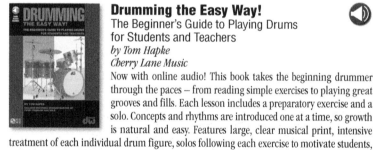

Drumming the Easy Way!
The Beginner's Guide to Playing Drums for Students and Teachers
by Tom Hapke
Cherry Lane Music
Now with online audio! This book takes the beginning drummer through the paces – from reading simple exercises to playing great grooves and fills. Each lesson includes a preparatory exercise and a solo. Concepts and rhythms are introduced one at a time, so growth is natural and easy. Features large, clear musical print, intensive treatment of each individual drum figure, solos following each exercise to motivate students, and more!
02500876 Book/Online Audio...$19.99
02500191 Book...$14.99

The Drumset Musician – 2nd Edition
by Rod Morgenstein and Rick Mattingly
Containing hundreds of practical, usable beats and fills, *The Drumset Musician* teaches you how to apply a variety of patterns and grooves to the actual performance of songs. The accompanying online audio includes demos as well as 18 play-along tracks covering a wide range of rock, blues and pop styles, with detailed instructions on how to create exciting, solid drum parts.
00268369 Book/Online Audio...$19.99

HAL•LEONARD®
www.halleonard.com

Instant Guide to Drum Grooves
The Essential Reference for the Working Drummer
by Maria Martinez
Become a more versatile drumset player! From traditional Dixieland to cutting-edge hip-hop, *Instant Guide to Drum Grooves* is a handy source featuring 100 patterns that will prepare working drummers for the stylistic variety of modern gigs. The book includes essential beats and grooves in such styles as: jazz, shuffle, country, rock, funk, New Orleans, reggae, calypso, Brazilian and Latin.
06620056 Book/CD Pack $12.99

1001 Drum Grooves
The Complete Resource for Every Drummer
by Steve Mansfield
Cherry Lane Music
This book presents 1,001 drumset beats played in a variety of musical styles, past and present. It's ideal for beginners seeking a well-organized, easy-to-follow encyclopedia of drum grooves, as well as consummate professionals who want to bring their knowledge of various drum styles to new heights. Author Steve Mansfield presents: rock and funk grooves, blues and jazz grooves, ethnic grooves, Afro-Cuban and Caribbean grooves, and much more.
02500337 Book..$14.99

Polyrhythms – The Musician's Guide
by Peter Magadini
edited by Wanda Sykes
Peter Magadini's *Polyrhythms* is acclaimed the world over and has been hailed by *Modern Drummer* magazine as "by far the best book on the subject." Written for instrumentalists and vocalists alike, this book with online audio contains excellent solos and exercises that feature polyrhythmic concepts. Topics covered include: 6 over 4, 5 over 4, 7 over 4, 3 over 4, 11 over 4, and other rhythmic ratios; combining various polyrhythms; polyrhythmic time signatures; and much more. The audio includes demos of the exercises and is accessed online using the unique code in each book.
06620053 Book/Online Audio..$19.99

Joe Porcaro's Drumset Method – Groovin' with Rudiments
Patterns Applied to Rock, Jazz & Latin Drumset
by Joe Porcaro
Master teacher Joe Porcaro presents rudiments at the drumset in this sensational new edition of *Groovin' with Rudiments*. This book is chock full of exciting drum grooves, sticking patterns, fills, polyrhythmic adaptations, odd meters, and fantastic solo ideas in jazz, rock, and Latin feels. The online audio features 99 audio clip examples in many styles to round out this true collection of superb drumming material for every serious drumset performer.
06620129 Book/Online Audio $24.99

66 Drum Solos for the Modern Drummer
Rock • Funk • Blues • Fusion • Jazz
by Tom Hapke
Cherry Lane Music
66 Drum Solos for the Modern Drummer presents drum solos in all styles of music in an easy-to-read format. These solos are designed to help improve your technique, independence, improvisational skills, and reading ability on the drums and at the same time provide you with some cool licks that you can use right away in your own playing.
02500319 Book/Online Audio...$17.99